KIDS ASK™
Why?

Illustrations by Tammie Lyon

Publications International, Ltd.

Why are flowers so colorful?

Why do bees sting?

Kids Ask is a trademark of Publications International, Ltd.

Copyright © 2007 Publications International, Ltd.
All rights reserved. This book may not be reproduced or quoted in whole
or in part by any means whatsoever without written permission from:

Louis Weber, CEO
Publications International, Ltd.
7373 North Cicero Avenue
Lincolnwood, Illinois 60712

Permission is never granted for commercial purposes.

ISBN-13: 978-1-4127-8945-5
ISBN-10: 1-4127-8945-1

Manufactured in China.

8 7 6 5 4 3 2 1

Contents

Why don't ducks get soaked?

Why is the lion called the king of beasts?

The lion is one of the largest animals in Africa. The male lion is known to be strong, powerful, and brave. It's also the only wild cat with a bushy, long mane around its neck and head. People in the past thought this made the lion look like a king wearing a crown.

Why are giraffes so tall?

A giraffe has a long neck and legs. Its neck can be more than ten feet long! (That's as long as a ladder.) Long legs and a long neck help the giraffe find food. It can reach tree leaves that no other animal can reach. A giraffe can also look over the trees and spot lions or other dangerous animals. Then it uses its long legs to run away!

FUN FACT
Some lions weigh as much as ten third graders!

Why don't boats sink?

Boats float because they are lighter than water. They are full of air, so even if the boat is huge and made of a heavy material such as steel, the air keeps it afloat. If the boat gets a leak and fills up with water, it will sink.

FUN FACT

Submarines need to sink. They pump enough water into hollow compartments around the boat to make it heavier than the surrounding water.

Why does the moon change shape?

The moon doesn't really change shape; it only looks that way to us. The moon reflects light from the sun. Sometimes the sun faces the moon and we see the whole, full moon. Other times the sun shines on one side of the moon and we see only part of it.

Why do owls come out at night?

Whooo can see in the dark? Whooo has very good hearing? Owls do! They put these skills to work at night, staying up to hunt mice and other small animals that come out to look for food.

FUN FACT

The tiniest owl is the *elf owl*, which is only five to six inches tall and weighs less than a hamburger!

Why do bees sting?

Bees don't sting anyone to be mean—they just use their stingers to protect themselves. Most people and animals know that many bees sting. We also know that getting stung by a bee hurts, so we stay away.

FUN FACT

The honey we eat comes from bees. Bees make honey to use as food, and bee farmers collect the honey that bees don't use and sell it to grocery stores all around the world.

Why are flowers so colorful?

Flowers are brightly colored to attract birds or insects. Birds and insects are important because they carry pollen from flower to flower to help create new flowers. Birds are often drawn to certain colors of flowers. Petals with spots on them may attract insects. The smells many flowers produce also attract insects.

Why does popcorn pop?

Inside each kernel of popcorn is water and something called *starch*. When the kernel gets very hot, the water turns to steam and the starch swells up. The starch gets so big it pops the hard shell—and you get a tasty treat!

FUN FACT

How high can popcorn pop? Up to three feet into the air!

Why do cats have whiskers?

Cats usually have 24 whiskers, 12 on each side of their face. Whiskers help tell cats about the world around them. If a twig or tough blade of grass touches the whiskers, cats will close their eyes to protect them from being poked. Cats can also use their whiskers to feel if there is enough room for them to fit through a tight space. They even use their whiskers to tell which way the wind is blowing.

Why do puppies sniff everything?

Dogs use their sense of smell to learn about the world around them. Because the world is new to them, puppies need to smell everything and everyone they meet.

FUN FACT

A dog's eyesight is worse than ours, but their sense of smell is so good that police officers use some kinds of dogs to track criminals and find missing people.

Why are there fire hydrants on the street?

A fire hydrant connects to underground pipes that carry water all over the city. When there is a fire, a fire truck hooks up to a hydrant near the fire. The truck pumps water from the hydrant into long hoses that the firefighters use to put the fire out.

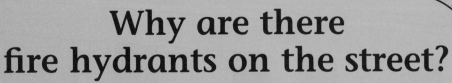

Why do police cars have flashing lights?

The flashing lights on a police car catch our attention even if we do not hear the police car's siren. The flashing lights tell drivers to pull over and stop.

FUN FACT

Some fire trucks have two steering wheels—one in the front and one in the back—so that firefighters can turn sharp corners on busy streets.

Why don't spiders get caught in their own webs?

Some of the threads in a web are sticky, and some are not. When an insect touches the web it gets stuck on the sticky part, and the spider runs down the non-sticky threads to get it.

Why do ants live in big groups?

Ants live and work together to survive. Some ants hunt for food, some build anthills, some have babies, and some care for the young. Ants help each other, and every ant has a chore to do.

FUN FACT

Ants can't see or hear very well, so they "talk" to each other by using smells. Ants leave a trail of smells to lead other ants to food. That's why you might see ants marching in a row toward your picnic basket.

Why do some trees change color in autumn?

Leaves appear green when the tree is using sunlight to make food (this is called *photosynthesis*). Many trees "sleep" during the winter when there isn't much sunlight, so they store up food all summer. When the fall comes and the tree doesn't need the leaves anymore, they lose the green color. When the green color disappears, other colors such as yellow, orange, and red are still there in the leaf.

Why do trees have bark?

Bark is really the "skin" of the tree. It protects the tree's trunk and branches from weather such as strong winds and extreme hot and cold. The bark on each tree grows in its own unique pattern, just like the fingerprints of a person.

Why do icicles hang from the roof?

When a winter day warms up a little, snow and ice on the roof start to melt and drip. When it turns cold enough to freeze again, the drips turn to ice. When this happens over and over, icicles are made.

FUN FACT

The largest snowflake ever recorded fell in Montana in 1887—it was bigger than a frying pan!

Why do we see our breath on a cold day?

here are very, very small droplets
f water in the air we breathe out.
hen our breath hits the cold air,
e droplets freeze and turn into a
ttle cloud, like a mini snowstorm!

23

Why do chimpanzees like to eat bananas?

Chimpanzees love fruit, and bananas are an especially sweet treat. It's easy for chimps to find bananas: They grow right there in the jungle, where wild chimps live. Plus, chimps have hands that are shaped almost like our own, with long fingers and a thumb that makes it easy for them to peel the yummy fruit.

FUN FACT

Before humans went into space, scientists sent animals. The first space chimpanzee was named Ham.

Why do gorillas pound their chest?

Sometimes gorillas pound their chest with their hands when they are excited. When a male gorilla thinks there is danger, he will pound on his chest and he may even throw things and break tree branches. He hopes this behavior will scare away whatever is threatening him. Gorillas don't pound on their chest to start fights. Gorillas are gentle. They just act tough.

Why don't ducks get soaked?

Ducks spend much of their time paddling around in the water, but they never look very wet. This is because they are covered in smooth feathers that overlap to keep the water out. Ducks make a special oil that they comb through their feathers with their beaks. This oil helps make the feathers waterproof, and the water runs off their bodies.

Why can't a turtle leave its shell?

A turtle's shell is part of its skeleton, just like your backbone is part of your skeleton. A turtle can pull its head and legs inside its shell for protection, but a turtle can't ever leave its shell.

FUN FACT

The largest turtle weighs as much as a cow!

Why are raisins wrinkled?

Raisins are grapes that have been dried. After the grapes are picked, they are laid out in the sun for about two weeks. As the grapes lose their moisture, they become wrinkled (and sweet!).

Why is thunder sometimes loud and sometimes quieter?

Thunder is made by lightning. When lightning is close by, the thunder is loud. When lightning is far away, the thunder is not as loud.

FUN FACT

A flash of lightning is hotter than the surface of the sun. If you see lightning in the sky, go inside your house right away!

Why do I need to sleep at night?

By the end of the day, you need a break! Sleep allows your body to rest and prepare for a new day. This time is like a mini vacation for your body and your brain. If you don't get enough sleep you may feel grouchy and tired. You may even feel confused or clumsy. It's especially important for children to get enough sleep so their bodies can grow. Sleep is necessary for your body to be strong and healthy. You won't get to sleep by bouncing on the bed! So lights out, and get some rest.